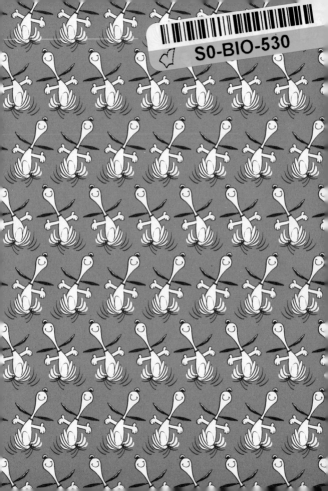

KEEP
CALM
AND DO THE
SNOOPY
DANCE

KEEP
CALM
AND DO THE
SNOOPY
DANCE

Charles M. Schulz

Andrews McMeel
Publishing®

Kansas City • Sydney • London

Peanuts is distributed internationally by Universal Uclick.

Andrews McMeel Publishing, LLC
an Andrews McMeel Universal company
1130 Walnut Street, Kansas City, Missouri 64106

www.andrewsmcmeel.com

15 16 17 18 19 TEN 10 9 8 7 6 5 4 3 2 1

ISBN: 978-1-4494-6864-4

Library of Congress Control Number: 2014952157

Attention: Schools and Businesses

Andrews McMeel books are available at quantity discounts with bulk purchase for educational, business, or sales promotional use. For information, please e-mail the Andrews McMeel Publishing Special Sales Department: specialsales@amuniversal.com.

KEEP
CALM
AND DO THE
SNOOPY
DANCE

There is a bit of insanity
in dancing that does everybody
a great deal of good.

— EDWIN DENBY

The sun does not shine
for a few trees and flowers,
but for the wide world's joy.

— HENRY WARD BEECHER

We're fools whether we dance or not, so we might as well dance.

— JAPANESE PROVERB

In three words I can sum up everything about life. It goes on.

— ROBERT FROST

Nobody cares if you
can't dance well.
Just get up and dance.

— DAVE BARRY

Let us dance in the sun,
wearing wild flowers in our hair.

— SUSAN POLIS SCHUTZ

Live in each season as it passes;
breathe the air, drink the drink,
taste the fruit.

— HENRY DAVID THOREAU

Everything in the universe
has rhythm. Everything dances.

— MAYA ANGELOU

To watch us dance
is to hear our hearts speak.

— HOPI INDIAN SAYING

Twenty years from now you
will be more disappointed by
the things that you didn't do
than the ones you did do.
So throw off the bowlines.
Sail away from the safe harbor.
Catch the trade winds in
your sails. Explore. Dream.
Discover.

— H. JACKSON BROWN, JR.

Happiness often sneaks in
through a door you didn't know
you left open.

— JOHN BARRYMORE

"Well," said Pooh, "what I like best—" and then he had to stop and think. Because although Eating Honey *was* a very good thing to do, there was a moment just before you began to eat it which was better than when you were, but he didn't know what it was called.

— A. A. MILNE

It's good to be just plain happy;
it's a little better to know that
you're happy; but to understand
that you're happy and to know
why and how . . . and still be
happy, be happy in the being and
the knowing, well that is beyond
happiness, that is bliss.

— HENRY MILLER

It's never too late to have
a happy childhood.

— TOM ROBBINS

The highest form of bliss is living
with a certain degree of folly.

— ERASMUS

Joy is a net of love by which
you can catch souls.

— **MOTHER TERESA**

My advice to you is not to
inquire why or whither,
but just enjoy your ice cream
while it's on your plate.

— **THORNTON WILDER**

Life is a great big canvas;
throw all the paint on it you can.

— **DANNY KAYE**

Let a joy keep you.
Reach out your hands
And take it when it runs by.

— **CARL SANDBURG**

When man is happy, he is
in harmony with himself
and his environment.

— OSCAR WILDE

Human beings, vegetables,
or cosmic dust, we all dance to
a mysterious tune, intoned in the
distance by an invisible player.

— ALBERT EINSTEIN

Life may not be the party we hoped for, but while we're here, we should dance.

— PROVERB

Will you, won't you, will you, won't you, will you join the dance?

— LEWIS CARROLL

Only when you drink from
the river of silence shall you
indeed sing. And when you
have reached the mountaintop,
then you shall begin to climb.
And when the earth shall
claim your limbs, then shall
you truly dance.

— KAHLIL GIBRAN

The one thing that you have
that nobody else has is *you*.
Your voice, your mind, your story,
your vision. So write and draw
and build and play and dance
and live as only you can.

— NEIL GAIMAN

There are shortcuts to happiness,
and dancing is one of them.

— **VICKI BAUM**

There is nothing to fear
except the persistent refusal to
find out the truth, the persistent
refusal to analyze the causes
of happenings. Fear grows
in darkness; if you think there's
a bogeyman around the corner,
turn on the light.

— DOROTHY THOMPSON

Find expression for a sorrow,
and it will become dear to you.
Find expression for a joy,
and you will intensify its ecstasy.

— OSCAR WILDE

If a man does not keep pace with his companions, perhaps it is because he hears a different drummer. Let him step to the music which he hears, however measured or far away.

— **HENRY DAVID THOREAU**

To dance is to be out of yourself.
Larger, more beautiful, more
powerful. This is power, it is
glory on earth and it is yours
for the taking.

— AGNES DE MILLE

Light tomorrow with today.

— ELIZABETH BARRETT BROWNING

Poetry is an echo,
asking a shadow to dance.

— **CARL SANDBURG**

The only way to make sense
out of change is to plunge into it,
move with it, and join the dance.

— ALAN WATTS

He that is of a merry heart
hath a continual feast.

— PROVERBS 15:15

Life is like dancing. If we
have a big floor, many people
will dance. Some will get angry
when the rhythm changes.
But life is changing all the time.

— **DON MIGUEL RUIZ**

I dance with the dancers.

— **WALT WHITMAN**

Mix a little foolishness with your serious plans. It is lovely to be silly at the right moment.

— **HORACE**

On with the dance!
Let joy be unconfined.

— LORD BYRON

ACTUALLY, I'M NEVER QUITE SURE JUST WHEN INDIAN SUMMER IS...SOME SAY IT'S THE WARM DAYS THAT FOLLOW THE FIRST FROST OF LATE AUTUMN..

ANYWAY, IT'S A NICE DAY, AND JUST IN CASE THIS IS INDIAN SUMMER, THIS IS MY INDIAN SUMMER DANCE!
SCHULZ

Those who dance are considered mad by those who hear not the music.

— PROVERB

We ought to dance with rapture
that we might be alive . . .
and part of the living,
incarnate cosmos.

— D. H. LAWRENCE

We should consider
every day lost on which we
have not danced at least once.

— **FRIEDRICH NIETZSCHE**

Dance is music made visible.

— **GEORGE BALANCHINE**

When you do dance, I wish you
A wave o' the sea, that you might
ever do
Nothing but that.

— WILLIAM SHAKESPEARE

And hand in hand, on the
edge of the sand,
They danced by the light of
the moon.

— EDWARD LEAR

Opportunity dances with those
already on the dance floor.

— H. JACKSON BROWN, JR.

We are all here for a spell; get all
the good laughs you can.

— **WILL ROGERS**

Do a loony-goony dance
'Cross the kitchen floor,
Put something silly in the world
That ain't been there before.

— SHEL SILVERSTEIN

I believe it is in my nature to dance by virtue of the beat of my heart, the pulse of my blood, and the music in my blood.

— ROBERT FULGHUM

I'd rather learn from one bird
how to sing than to teach ten
thousand stars how not to dance.

— E. E. CUMMINGS

Discover day-to-day excitement.

— **CHARLES BAUDELAIRE**

To me, the body says
what words cannot.

— MARTHA GRAHAM

Life is the dancer
and you are the dance.

— ECKHART TOLLE

The joyful heart sees and reads
the world with a sense
of freedom and graciousness.

— **JOHN O'DONOHUE**

Dance, even if you have nowhere
to do it but your living room.

— MARY SCHMICH

Every day brings a chance
for you to draw in a breath,
kick off your shoes,
and step out and dance.

— OPRAH WINFREY

Don't hurry, don't worry.
You're only here for a short visit.
So be sure to stop and
smell the flowers.

— WALTER HAGEN

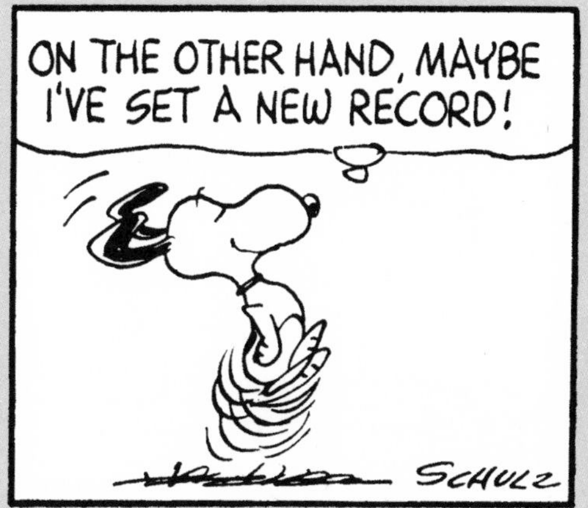
ON THE OTHER HAND, MAYBE I'VE SET A NEW RECORD!
SCHULZ

Dancing can reveal all the
mystery that music conceals.

— **CHARLES BAUDELAIRE**

When you dance, your purpose
is not to get to a certain place
on the floor. It's to enjoy
each step along the way.

— WAYNE DYER

To watch the corn grow, and the blossoms set; to draw hard breath over ploughshare or spade; to read, to think, to love, to pray—these are the things that make us happy.

— JOHN RUSKIN

You must understand the whole
of life, not just one little part of it.
That is why you must read,
that is why you must look at the
skies, that is why you must sing
and dance, and write poems,
and suffer, and understand,
for all that is life.

— J. KRISHNAMURTI

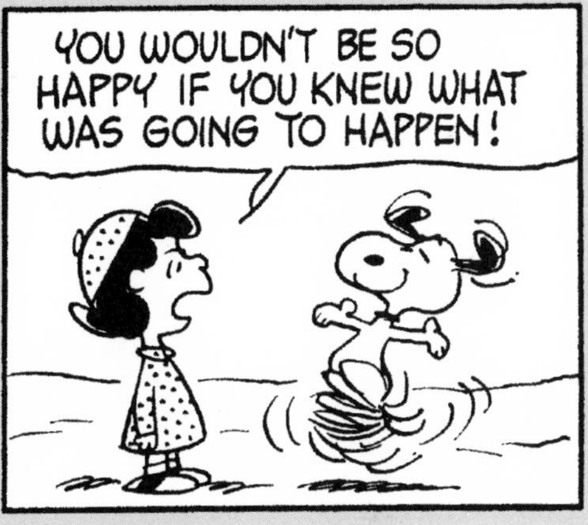
YOU WOULDN'T BE SO HAPPY IF YOU KNEW WHAT WAS GOING TO HAPPEN!

Life is what we make it,
always has been, always will be.

— **GRANDMA MOSES**

Dancing is silent poetry.

— **SIMONIDES**

Look, I really don't want to wax philosophic, but I will say that if you're alive, you got to flap your arms and legs, you got to jump around a lot, you got to make a lot of noise, because life is the very opposite of death.

— **MEL BROOKS**

While I dance I cannot judge,
I cannot hate, I cannot separate
myself from life. I can only
be joyful and whole.
This is why I dance.

— HANS BOS

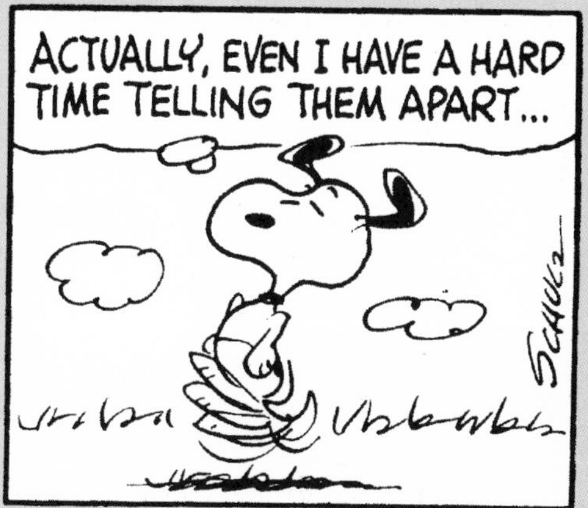
ACTUALLY, EVEN I HAVE A HARD TIME TELLING THEM APART...
SCHULZ

Dance till the stars come down from the rafters; Dance, dance, dance till you drop.

— W. H. AUDEN

For myself, I am an optimist—
it does not seem to be much use
being anything else.

— **WINSTON CHURCHILL**

The more in harmony with
yourself you are, the more joyful
you are, and the more faithful
you are. Faith is not to disconnect
you from reality—it connects
you to reality.

— PAULO COELHO

There is only the dance.

— T. S. ELIOT

I have a simple philosophy.
Fill what's empty.
Empty what's full.
And scratch where it itches.

— **ALICE ROOSEVELT LONGWORTH**

Never dance in a puddle
when there's a hole in your shoe
(it's always best to take your
shoes off first).

— JOHN D. RHODES

Joy is what happens to us when
we allow ourselves to recognize
how good things really are.

— **MARIANNE WILLIAMSON**

Every day that is born into
the world comes like a burst
of music, and rings itself all
the day through; and thou
shalt make of it a dance, a dirge,
or a life march as thou wilt.

— THOMAS CARLYLE

Dance is so joyous.

— GRAEME MURPHY

Let us go singing as far as we go;
the road will be less tedious.

— VIRGIL

If you want to be happy, be.

— **LEO TOLSTOY**

Music and rhythm find their way
into the secret places of the soul.

— **PLATO**

Dancing is the loftiest,
the most moving, the most
beautiful of the arts, because
it is no mere translation or
abstraction from life;
it is life itself.

— HAVELOCK ELLIS

You should be dancing.

— THE BEE GEES